Beneath the Sheets...
Above the Comforter

by

Sheri Celada

Soul Asylum
Poetry and Publishing Inc.

© Copyright 2013 Sheri Celada
All rights reserved.
No part of this publication may be reproduced, stored in a retrieval system, or transmitted, in any form or by any means, electronic, mechanical, photocopying, recording, or otherwise, without the written prior permission of the author.
Note for Librarians: a cataloguing record for this book that includes Dewey Decimal Classification and US Library of Congress numbers is available from the Library and Archives of Canada. The complete
cataloguing record can be obtained from their online database at:
www.collectionscanada.ca/amicus/index-e.html
ISBN# 978-1-926876-41-2

Published in Canada by Soul Asylum Poetry
79 De La Salle Blvd, Jackson's Point, ON L0E 1L0
www.soulasylumpoetry.com

Cover Art Design: Steven Gastis
Illustrations: Sheldon Wheatley
Project Editor: Kenneth William Cowle

Soul Asylum
Poetry and Publishing Inc.

10 9 8 7 6 5 4 3 2 1

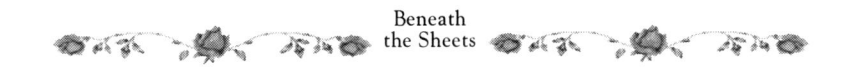

Dedicated to Karen Arney

Your beautiful loving nature touched so many and always made them smile. Your gentle voice and hands always found the way to console ones heart. You accepted everything and made the best out of even the smallest things.

They always say great things come in small packages and yet you had a huge heart.

Thank you for helping me become the person I am today and for understanding me as I grew.

I thank you for the breath of life and for believing in me even when I didn't. I know that you continue to watch over me and guide me in my choices.

I will always carry you in my heart and never forget you. My love for you will never stop and I will always miss you.
I am very proud to call you "MOM".

Table of Contents

The One	1
Unspoken Love	2
Yellow Rose	3
Why A Child?	4
Angelic White Knight	6
God's Little Angel	7
A Dream In Motion	8
A Gift Beyond Beauty	9
More Then Just One Night	10
Eternity	12
Beneath The Skin	13
You Make The World A Better Place	14
A Heart In Limbo	15
I Thought I Lost It	16
A Jewel From The Heavens	17
A Precious Gift	18
A Simple Person	19
A Treasure You Do Share	20
Across The Miles	21
An Angel Has Been Sent To Me	22
An Angel's Soul	23
Eyes Of A Rose	24
Flickering Flames	25
Friends From Heaven	26
God's Calling	27
God's Choice	28
Hungry Heart	29
I'm Sorry	30
Journey From Within	31
Message With A Rose	32
On The Wings Of A Friend	33
On Mother's Wings	34
Please Release Me	36
The Board	37
Simplicity Of One	38
The Chosen One	40

Table of Contents

The Heaven Above 41
The Lord's Eagle 42
The Puzzle Of Life 43
The Twisted Tongue 44
Unspoken Beauty 45
Precious Moments 46
Cinderella 48
My Masterpiece 49
The Mirror 50
The Man I Love 51
A Nightmare 52
A Lover Like No Other 54
The Angel In All Of Us 55
Fulfilled But Curious 56
To Love Him Is To Dream 57
Erotic Passion 58
Little 8 Cylinder Camero 59
You Don't Understand 60
Sisters 61
Parenting 62
A Mishap 63
Running Doesn't Help 64
As Good As Gold 65
Who's There 66
Two Becoming One 67
If Tomorrow Never Comes 68

Acknowledgements

Thank you to everyone who has believed and supported me over the years of writing. Those who encouraged me to keep writing and expressed their feedback about the writings I had already done. Many of you have been an inspiration to me and brought meaning to the words I have written, without you this book may not be here today.

I wanted to say never give up on your dreams as you never know what tomorrow will bring nor what you can do unless you try it. Believe in yourself and remember the true beauty is in your heart & soul.

Appreciation and thanks go out to Ken Cowle of Soul Asylum Poetry and Publishing for all of your hard work and dedication to the artists who fill the playground and airwaves. You have overcome a lot but always stayed strong and maintained a safe venue for us to express ourselves.
http://www.soulasylumpoetry.com

Paths cross for many different reasons in life and I am truly grateful for the positive energy that has been given to me from so many of you. There may not always be enough hours in every day or maybe there is just too many miles that keep us apart but please know I appreciate you all and carry you in my heart. Thank you for making a difference in my life.

Energy and speed is no stranger to a woman who is a wonderful inspiration to so many. Someone who shows that if you believe, you will achieve. She continues to be passionate about life, family and career but yet still strong and determined as she strives in a "man's sport". Isabelle Tremblay is a determined woman who continues to reach for the checker flag both on and off the track. Thank you for never giving up.
http://www.isaracingteam.com

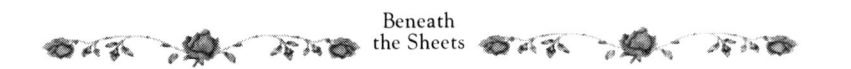

The One

Your lips bless my ears with passion
Your heart soars to mine
Our giggles intertwine
With our words embracing each other

Through the hours we dream a little stronger each time
Our hearts open and our eyes closed
Visions of each other's embrace form
To the heavens we soar

The candles and cuddles
Or the rose petals surrounding us
The pallet of the rainbow has filled our hearts
Together we soar

Unspoken Love

The Lord's creation of purity
The Heavens Angel of love and beauty
A rainbow's pallet of colour within heart and soul
The tongue of passion and romance

Touch of depth beneath the layers of skin
Soaring within my dreams and taking me higher then the skies itself
Penetrating through my heart and staying deep
Your name blessing my lips and giggles

Closing my eyes your hands touch mine and lock us together
Your smile so prominent and beautiful
A song playing loud and clear but yet not from any radio or stereo
Your key unlocks my heart and mine unlocks yours

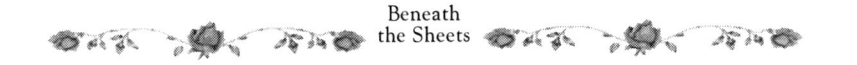

Yellow Rose

High above the heavens is where you rest
Through the rainbows you keep watch
Their steps, their breaths
You hear them all

As the rainbow brightens it is you smiling
The mist that falls is your tears of happiness
For you share in their every move
You glorify while they live

Your love sits within their hearts
Your smile rests in their soul
Memories strengthen their every step
Blessed are they

You have answered your calling
Open the gates and spread the beauty
The treasures you have granted earth
So sacred and genuine

May you rest in peace
Know that you are never forgotten
Always loved and treasured
Your glory shines here within your loved ones

Why A Child

*There he lay listening and watching
So attentive and curious
Almost as if he knew
Knew what was being said*

*Questions he would ask
Then the words would continue
So attentively he did listen
He cuddled and kissed
Told Mommy he loved her*

Why a child

*As we finished the coat of many colour
His precious little voice spoke
Mommy why do I have a book about God
My lips and my heart were frozen
I was speechless*

*Those words were just the first
The next few minutes got even harder
He turned to me with tear filled eyes
He asked about Nanny and God
He explained God did not give Nanny her wings
Nanny did it herself*

Why a child

*My heart skipped a beat
I hoped I could do this
When Nanny went to heaven
God opened the gates and welcomed her in
He showed her around and let her pick her wings*

God gave her instructions on how to use the wings
He reflected back
Nanny visited him at night
His doodle board directed her
His eyes still tear filled

Why a child

His sweet words flowed
With such innocence
Looking for the answers
Yet his heart and mind seemed set

He asked Mommy who loves me
We spoke of a list of people who loved him
Including God and his best new buddy

Why a child

Angelic White Knight

*Threw the heavens and across the ocean's ripples
Your glow illuminates the air and fills the pallet
of the rainbow
Your strength nurtures the seeds that hunger in the fields
The depth of your soul strengthens
the birds' wings to fly higher*

*Across the sand children's faces glow and
their innocent hearts sing
Your compassion and genuine heart purify
them and light their paths to dreams
Distinction and tenderness of a rose's petal
is held in your hands
The breath beneath your lips ignites the fire within the souls*

*The flames never grow cold or dim
For the precious gift you share burns eternally
You will live within our hearts forever and the love we have
for you will never die*

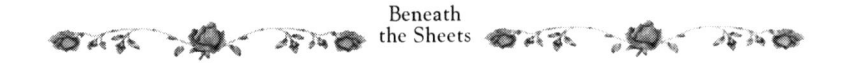

God's Little Angel

Pretty in pink with a braid to the side
Your soft voice told me a story
My heart felt your pain
Apart it broke, and I shared your pain

As my eyes crystallized
The surroundings disappeared
I looked into your sorrowed eyes
A prayer released to the heavens

As I close my eyes I see you
There you lay in your chair
Bandages surrounding your wounds
Pain in your shouts

I wish I could
Just one day awake all well again
We separated in the halls
But the vision of you
Stayed in my heart

A Dream In Motion

Closing the eyes I remember
You walking down the ramp
The smile that was attached to it
And the kind voice that followed

You were tired and frustrated
But this did not stop your kindness
The smiles flowed freely
And the tension was forgotten

To close them again I hold the vision
Of laughter and freedom
The availability to be ourselves
The invention of the dance

Listening in the wind I hear laughter
And see the smiles that accompanied that laughter
The tape that allowed us to chuckle
The fear of embarrassment disappeared

Sharing in the portrait that did lay on the building
A breath taking view
To hear you breathe the inspiration to those around you
My heart id did beat to the rhythm

My heart and soul do hear a lot still
I hold it close and smile
Though to close the eyes one more time
You catch the tears sliding down the cheek

Finding the words to say goodbye and thank you
Sharing the last few moments and the embraces
Looking up I see you walking but never turning
The silence overtook the air

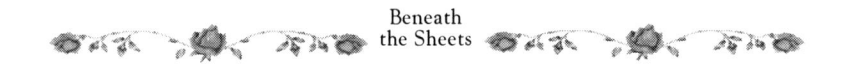

A Gift Beyond Beauty

*My heart has motion again
The soul knows how to believe
The lips know how to smile again
Eyes sparkle and shine*

*Feel the breeze that has blown in
The breeze of warmth and appreciation
Inspiration and support
A feeling like no other*

*Words seem to fall short
Short of explaining the appreciation within the heart
Not at once have you been taken for granted
You are always appreciated and never forgotten*

*A prayer to the heavens above
To help me find the perfect treasure for you
A treasure to bless you the way you blessed others
A gift beyond beauty for you*

*To move mountains for you
Or to light the rainbows in the sky as you awaken
Laying the brightest stars over you when you sleep
Offering the beauty back to you*

More Than Just One Night

*More than just one night
I close my eyes and there you are
Within my thoughts, within my heart
It seems so real*

*The tender caress
The passionate kiss
Embrace to ecstasy
Within the warmth of your arms*

*The world around disappears
Cherished is the moment
Long and passionate
Warm and real*

*Even when I open my eyes
You surround my thought
Make me smile and wish it was now
You've taken me to Heaven and back*

*Do you feel me thinking of you
Do my whispers make it to you*

The stars are ours to count

Beneath
the Sheets

11

Eternity

The praise unto you and the pride I hold for you
Eternal gift and unconditional love
The white rose lying upon your pillow
accompanying a note of love
The most precious Angel came to life
the day you were born

Eternally thanking the Lord
for your unconditional love
Your undying beauty illuminates the world
more then any ray of light ever could

Sharing unto you the honor I feel in your presence
and the pride for you I have
Within your heart and soul is where I want to stay
and in your arms forever

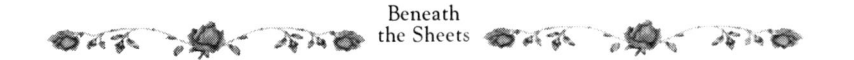

Beneath The Skin

*As you parasite through my life
My heart cascades to pieces
My eyes crystallize
My soul bruises*

*Within the shell like walls I did live
Living through a crack to the outside
Wanting to know more
Wanting to breath freely and live*

*Shattered the shell does lye
The beauty I did smell
The songs of Heaven I did hear
Blessings I did receive*

You Make The World A Better Place

You've been an Angel to the world
You're heart and soul has rocked us from within
You've touched our heart beyond expression
All because of the YOU, the world is a brighter place

Your smile and sincerity light the days brighter then the sun
Your unique inner beauty illuminates the skies
beyond the stars
Your soul is the banner for the Heavens high
God chose the best man and he was YOU

Your genuine intuition and strength
has measured up to mountains
Your gentleness and inner beauty has surpassed
any rose ever grown
The compassion and love you possess
is better then any Hallmark card
Your talent and tongue for music glorifies us all

You make a difference in our lives
and yet upon our heart your imprints lye
Our thoughts and prayers fill of you,
thanks given to the Lord for each breath with you
The Angels to watch over you
and shelter you from harm, to keep you safe
You are always a blessing from above, please don't change

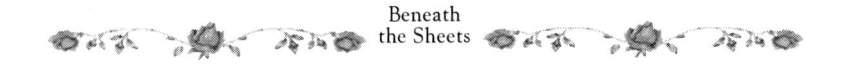

A Heart In Limbo

*If ever I knew what to do with this heart
It came with no instructions
It was marked fragile, handle with care
But yet it seems so tough*

*It is very BIG and golden in colour
Though if you look closely
You will see a lot of bruises
Those areas have just become stronger*

A heart in limbo, with no where to go

*It has been stepped over, and walked on
Turned inside out
Somehow it still holds life
It finds the way to beat on*

*No matter how it was shattered or torn
It never skipped a beat
It has been empty and cold
As well as full and warm*

A heart in limbo, with no where to go

*It gets confused at times
Finds itself searching for direction
Sometimes even hitting dead ends
Or doors that are locked to this heart*

*It often pours too much too strong
It really means no harm
It is just too caring*

A heart in limbo, with no where to go

I Thought I Lost It

I hear a calling
A calling from up high
Up above the turn
The path is shining

Direction has been given
He has allowed me back
Actually he has never shut the doors
My spot has always been there

I thought I lost it but it was always in my heart

I swayed from the path a bit
But I never forgot
I remembered what I had to do
And why I am who I am

I remembered how to speak
And how to listen
I faced a lot of challenges
Over came them all somehow

I thought I lost it but it was always in my heart

Still life can be a challenge
But I believe
The prayers, the words
The strength that has been given

A rainbow lines the sky
A blessing fills the heart and soul
To know the truth now
He never locked me out

I thought I lost it but it was always in my heart

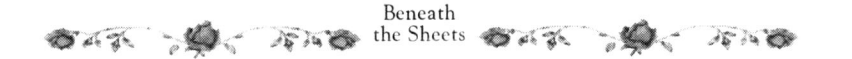

A Jewel From The Heavens

*You have inspired me
Like the heavens have inspired you
You have brightened my world
Like the sun brightens the day*

*You have taught my heart how to beat again
Like a child learning how to take the first steps
You have allowed me to feel beauty
Like the soil allows the rose to breath*

*You have allowed me to smile repeatedly
Like the sparkle of a jewel
You have shared and trusted in me
Like HE did with his disciples*

*You have shared something so precious
A friendship without doubt or prejudice
How does one say Thank You
For the inner beauty you have shared*

*My heart reaches out to you
In hopes of repaying your kindness and generosity
To allow your world to shine
Just like you have mine*

A Precious Gift

As we open up each others eyes to life and friendship
We bond closer and tighter together
Yet so far apart in miles across the globe

A special person like you will never be forgotten
One day the lord may cross our paths physically
But for now he has chosen other ways to bond us

Offering up thanks for a friend like you
Praise to the Lord for trusting me with your well being

I hold a key to your heart and you a key to mine
The door will never lock us out
No matter what the hour or day
No need to knock first
Enter in confidence and blessings

I thank the Lord for sending me YOU

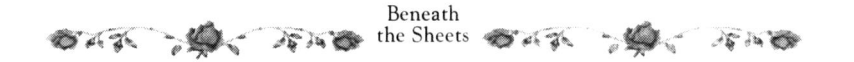

A Simple Person

*I have heard your calling
This calling I have answered
You have blessed me with so much
How could I ever repay you*

*You have removed the blinders
I can see again
Always have I been a simple person
Simplicity speaks a lot*

*I hold the hearts of others high to the heavens
There I shelter them and protect against evil
Nothing in return do I ask
They hold precedence above my own*

*To help them smile again
Wiping their tears away and warding off their fears
Allowing the to see their inner beauty
To believe in themselves once again*

*Sentimental and romantic I have been
To those whom want to listen
Though many don't understand
It is not a beat everyone wants to hear*

*Spontaneity and romance I do hold
My heart contains a lot waiting to share
But though, I am just me
A simple person*

A Treasure You Do Share

HE descended down upon me
Whispered in my ear
To this treasure you do cherish
You have been given a gift of beauty

I closed my eyes and paused
Whispers from my heart HE did receive
A heartfelt Thank You
And a promise to continue on the path

My heart and soul you have mended
You have allowed me to believe again
To see all beauty and feel all blessings
This itself is a treasure

A blessing you have shared with me
Something like no other
No words could ever describe
The way this has made me feel

The inner me have strengthened
The heart and soul so free to share again
Obstacles I have jumped
Learned to walk again

The heavens have heard my dreams
You have blessed me from high above
A treasure you have granted me
I do so cherish

I promise to keep this treasure you do share
Close to my heart and sheltered from pain
To show my appreciation and praise
Until all of eternity

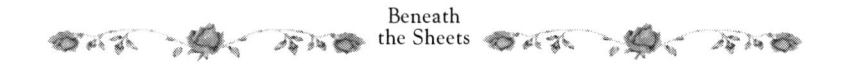

Across The Miles

You built your life out of bricks
They stacked higher each day
The truth you locked and sheltered
Deeper then a pirate's treasure

Your calling was not heard
So quiet you stayed
You assumed life was meant to be that way
But when really inside you were screaming

You had questions of life
You wanted to be heard
Let alone you wanted to be loved
You wanted to be special

Though all along you were that
You have been special the whole time
Many lost an opportunity of a lifetime
A marvelous chance to know YOU

From across the miles your wall did shatter
You stepped out into the light
Looked in the mirror and saw the beauty
A beauty you have hid within for years

Your calling was heard and your answer granted
You were sheltered the entire puzzle of life
But now you step your own steps
And release the gift you have

An Angel has been sent to us

Here we stand together
The coldest day in 50 years
Your smile warms the world
And your spirit shelters us

The words of wisdom ring out
The ears listen
The eyes watch
The smiles follow
Another door has been unlocked

An Angel has been sent to us

As the journey comes to an end
The butterflies swim and the tears fall
The memories of yesterday
So warm in our hearts
Memories that will never be forgotten

A dream has become realization
Our lives touched
Yet in so many ways
Our hearts have not stop singing
With hope you have heard them

An Angel has been sent to us

As you soar high in the sky
Our thoughts and prayers follow you
No matter how high you stand
No matter where you stand
Or under what name
You will never be forgotten

An Angel has been sent to us

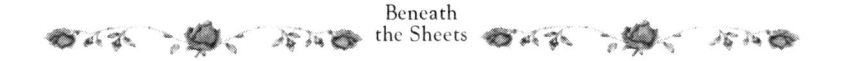

An Angel's Soul

*You soared across the skies above
Chased the dark clouds away
You wiped the dust from on the rainbow
Where countless colour did shine*

*Storms from within my heart you did catch
Showers of tears from abroad you did wipe
You watered the rose and lit the flame
Restoration of truth you did offer*

*With your eyes you have seen my dreams
With your soul you have heard my heart
With your heart you have felt my tears
With your smile you have brightened the path*

*Blessed is this gift I receive of you
A masterpiece of genuine beauty
A glory of inspiration
An eternal torch burning within me*

*Your flame is always lit
Never will a wind be able to blow it out
For the strength it does offer
My soul it does glorify*

Eyes Of A Rose

The sand on the beach
The beauty of the sunset
All a dream to me
So far from my touch in reality

To one it matters not
It makes no sense why
What the value it holds
To me I know those answers

Beauty is what you make of it
How you treat it
Heart and soul leads to inner beauty
Symbols of nature leading to beauty

No one understands
A different angle we do share
An appreciation seen through eyes unknown
An understanding from within

A breath, a smile, a tear
Nothing taken for granted
Beauty is seen, felt and heard
The loss of it can happen at any time

Clear the eyes that view the world
Absorb and appreciate while it lasts
Give thanks for even the smallest of things
Live life to the fullest, dare to dream

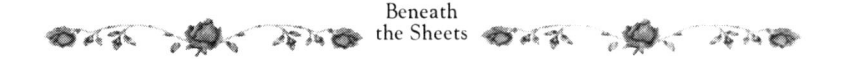

Flickering Flames

*Words grazing the tender lips
Whispers of the heart echoing in the air
Gentleness of the hand lay upon the other
Stroke of the hair and a golden smile*

*Chocolate covered strawberries and champagne
Soft rose petals lay abroad and teddies take place beside
Long stem red rose lies within your hands
Ambiance amongst the room as the music plays
and the candles flicker*

*The breath brushes the check and warms the ear
One hand intertwines amongst the other
Within each other's arms we circle
Our hearts simultaneously beat*

*Together our hearts sing such beauty
Warmth surrounds us as we wrap within each other's arms
With the head upon your chest I gaze into
the flickering flames
Within me, I know this is where I want to be*

Friends From Heaven

*Without question you opened your heart
The pages shared your story
Between the lines I read the beauty
We shared the laughs and tears*

*Beyond the words were meanings of truth and support
Unconditional love for each other
A sister, a brother, a treasure of my heart
A beauty beyond words*

*What heavens did open up and bless me with this
A difference in my heart and soul
Truth of my dreams and direction in my journey
Two paths crossed and opened up a whole new one*

*Pages of our lives we do share
Walls we do climb together and catch each other when we fall
Respect and appreciation we do share
Your heart and soul holds something so precious*

*Your genuine self is a treasure I thank you for sharing
A walk in your life is a blessing
The back will never turn and the ears always open
The hand right there for the grasping*

*You have warmed my heart and soul
Touched my life and rocked my world
Within those steps we walk beside each other
Acceptance of the inner truth and a love of the real you*

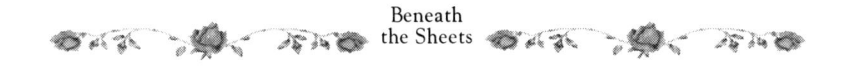

God's Calling

*You called your next angel
And she answered
She loved us here on earth
But she loved them in heaven too
Though our hearts broke apart
The fight we fought but did not win*

*The victory we did hold
Was the victory of peace
The knowing of no more pain to you
The comfort of you watching over us
Guiding each of your loved ones
Each and every step*

*The emptiness in our hearts
The emptiness in your chair
Never will be filled by anyone else
But knowing your love
We know you will never stop loving
Loving us, all of us who have been your life*

*There you soar with God
High above the skies
But still never too high for me to say
Mommy I love you with all my heart
I will never forget you*

Sheri Celada

God's Choice

God smiles every night before bed
When he looks down on you and your journeys
He sends down the brightest star
To sit outside your window
In case you wanted to wish upon it
And the brightest moon
To guide you across the boardwalk at night

God knew you wee perfect inside
When he handed down to you the powers you hold
And the inspirational blessings you lay upon the world
He made his choice and he's never regret it since this day

He knows the staff was handed to the correct person
In time you have learned how to use it
With even more still to learn
Your spirit and positive energy enlightens this world
So much that it could be mistaken for Heaven
It is beautiful here with you

Even the roses as gentle as they be
Hold no beauty against you
This beauty is within
A treasure no one can replace

The Lord heard our prayers
He searched high and low
Blessed us with a jewel
A jewel of inspiration

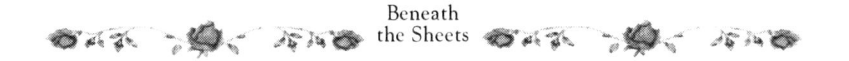

Hungry Heart

The eyes of a rose, always seeing the beauty of it all
Golden heart encased with millions of footprints
Dreams from within, frozen in time
Inner self hidden and out of touch

Young, anxious, and ambitious
Offering all and never questioning
Eager to sow the oats of friendships
The threads of romance

Above and beyond my heart did lead me
The eagerness to please and perfect
Wanting to feel the gift everyone else had
The gift of being loved

Turning all the corners and sharing the shadows
Having the feet wiped upon my heart and soul
My eyes so sealed I couldn't see
My heart sang to a melody unknown to the soul

Tricks and tribulations did surround me
Behind the closed doors the tears shed and the heart bled
The truth locked so deep within and the key thrown away
Tomorrow was another day and the urge was back

Though the paths may have led to different corners
The footsteps I did take
Circles of life did not evolve at the time
The heart was hungry for love

I'm Sorry

Upon the lips there rests
A few words that always release
They seem to find their way out
No matter what

I guess the heart is convinced
Those are the words that it is so used to
They have been said a lot as years gone by
No matter where the fault fell
Almost like a second nature

It seems to come naturally
Nothing planned or in script
I believe the heart doesn't know otherwise
It has had to say it so many times
Many of which it shouldn't have
But being the heart it is
You tend to hear it a lot

The heart will try to understand
There is no need to say it
Unless the fault is due
These words are not said to irritate
But the heart knows no other

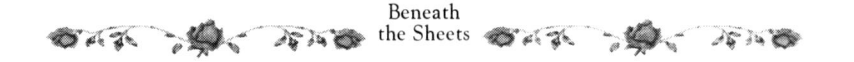

Journey From Within

Oh Lord, I can speak again
The tongue is not swallowed
The voice box not broken
The passage clear and open

The words return to the soul
Inspired and enlightened
The heart mended
As golden as can be

The eyes they can see
A beauty shown to me
Beyond the shell there lies a truth
Waiting to be explored

The footprints I do follow
Are deep and permanent
A message to understand and trust
The colour of the soul is like a rainbow

A beauty of a butterfly
Softness of a rose
Innocence of a baby
The road I have choose

No more doubting within myself
The confirmation I do hold
The path is clear
And the journey has begun

Message With A Rose

Across the moon lit beach
Amongst the water ripples
The tranquil sand beneath the feet
A distinguished vision appears

The light glistens across the waters
And grazes the sand, accenting the footprints
The footprints lay across the beach
Blessing the earth with such grace

The prints lead to the waters
With a single red rose remaining
A note strikes your eyes on the stem
Unfolded it lay in your hands

You strive to read it amongst
the tears glistening from your eyes
Etched in ink you read the words " You are Loved "
You bow your head and then raise your
crystal eyes to the heavens
The clouds separate and the
moon shines down upon the water

A shooting star pierces the silence of the sky
Within your heart you feel the warmth
He has spoken to you
You have received Him within

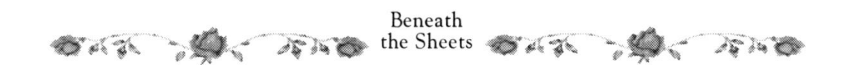

On The Wings Of A Friend

As your tears flow
The heart breaks
Hours seems like decades
And the eyes cannot close

Races of memories
Yet questions beyond answers
Your mind is working overtime
Trying to find peace is hard

Remember the sunshine days
The rainbows she brought with her
The laughs you shared
Yet how you complimented each other

As she rests in peace
Hear her breath to you
Feel the message within your heart
You are never forgotten

She will stand beside you every step
Fill your heart when it seems empty
Though she has risen to the Lord
She is always within you

On Mother's Wings

Brown hair so fine and simple
Blue eyes of sparkling crystals
Voice of soft and gentle
Heart full and giving

You gave me the most precious gift
The gift of life and love
You loved me unconditionally
My tears you heard and wiped

The sketches of unknown you treasured
Every project was special to you
I was special to you
You taught me a lot and I will never forget

You held my hand more then once and listened to my dreams
Your love for life I admired even on the toughest days
Whether stitching buttons or my heart you always had time
Together we laughed and lived

You were there for my firsts and lasts
No matter the day you always found a smile for me
A gentle image that I will never forget
Your place is always in my heart and soul

You have lit my paths since your journey took you far away
Beside me I know you do walk
You keep watch over me
and often whisper to me from the heavens
Your beauty will always remain precious and treasured

Beneath
the Sheets

Please Release Me

The pallet of my dreams
Pale and empty
The beating of my heart
Quiet and withdrawn

My soul, alone and timid
The walk, long and unknown
Beauty I know and feel
Frozen and far from the touch

Life, a circle of unknown
Not always fair
The tunnels look dark at both ends
The rainbows at a loss of colour

Every falling star, I do wish upon
I pray someone hears me
And feels my tears
The days grow long and the nights short

I search for the key
The key to unlock my life
To release it from the chambers of unknown
To light the candle and find my way

My wings, crinkled and tarnished
I want to spread them wide
I want to take flight into life
Please release me from this unknown

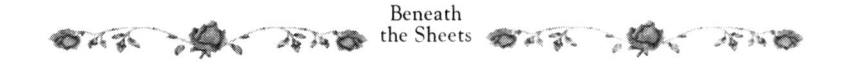

The Board

*Here we sit behind a screen
A family spread across the world
So many words we share
Our bonds form
And our hearts warm*

*Many nights and days
We spend in here
Posting from our hearts
And sharing our dreams*

*Opening the doors to new members
Offering our hand
And stretching out our arms
Opening our ears and hearts
Sharing our blessings*

*A family many would never understand
Yet to those who are here
We know and understand the bonds
A cherished gift we all share
A blessing from up above*

*Here we all stand together as one
Becoming stronger each and every day
Spreading our wings
Carrying the words across the world
Standing strong for that which we believe*

*A family we have joined
A friendship bond we have formed
Not just "A Board "
But yet a home we will cherish*

Simplicity Of One

Not a super model walk
Or a Hollywood smile
My pockets are not green
But my heart is gold

The clothes not branded
Jewels do not surround me
Look within my soul
Hear the meaning of my words

Walk the rainbow with me
Inspire through the colour
Close your eyes and dreams
Allow the clouds to sculpt in front of you

Smile the rays of sunshine
Giggle and laugh the sounds of angels
Breathe the flight of an eagle
Feel the purity of a dove

Reach higher then the mountaintops
Spread your wings and soar free
Look within your heart and soul
See what is so obvious but yet hidden

Beneath
the Sheets

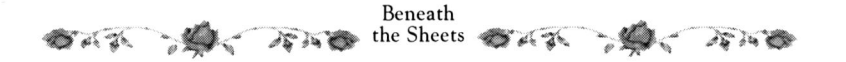

The Chosen One

You hold the holy book
And wear the symbolic pendulum
You spread your wings
And by the most beautiful blessings

Your words of inspiration
Your smile trust and comfort
Blessings from one soul to another
Nothing tangible do you ask

You glorify in the smiles of those you reach
To feed the hungry with your soul
To teach them how to believe again

Footprints of yours you see forever
Impressions of your journeys
Are imbedded in those you have met
Within their hearts and souls

You may physically leave
But you will always be there
You will never be forgotten
And yet always welcomed back

You are rewarded inspirationally for this
Your heart and soul fill with the love
The love you are blessed with from one and all
Young or old you touch them all

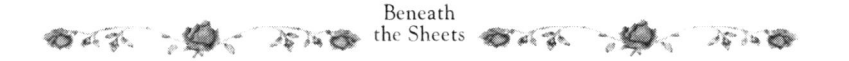

The Heavens Above

I stumbled and you caught me
I cried, you wiped my tears
I felt I was alone and you reminded me otherwise
I needed someone to listen and you were there

You always found a way to smile upon me
You offered me direction
You offered me challenges
I listened, and I heard your words

When I forgot my ways you found me
When I doubted you understood
When the corner looked like home
You comforted me and brought me out

You sit upon my heart and within my soul
I whisper to you every day
Sometimes every hour
Maybe not in such fancy words

I watch your heavens shift and shape from down below
Close my eyes and imagine the inner beauty
Pray that the day my calling comes
You accept me into your world, your family

The Lord's Eagle

Whether you soar like an eagle
Or swim like a dolphin
Your heart and soul
The pure beauty they do hold
Words of inspiration and wisdom
Your lips do release

Gold, silver or none
This does not matter to the true heart
Fancy labels or stamped on logos
Branded names do not matter
Jewels, money and fancy cars
They don't inspire either

Inside you is what matters
Your heart and soul
The real YOU
Your friendship, your trust
The respect you hold for me
The bond we share
No jewel could measure to this

My back it never does turn on you
My ears always those to listen
Shoulders always there for you to lean on
My heart always there to care
My eyes always open to see you are human
A smile to welcome and cheer you

The hand is always open
The arm is extended
When you are ready
Reach out, I will be here

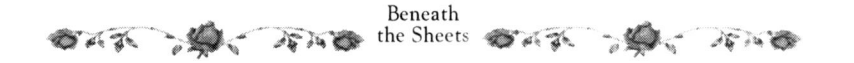

The Puzzle Of Life

Life is such a precious gift
We tend to take it for granted
A smile something beautiful
But yet lost from most

To simply giggle uncontrollably
To blush a few shades of red
To be the most precious gift
Just being YOU

The key to the heart tends to break
The lock seizes and we forget
We forget how to let ourselves feel
How to feel special and beautiful

The sun is free to shine
The stars free to twinkle
Our hearts are imprisoned
The heart cries out to be heard
Will someone please release it

We look up high
Take a moment of silence
Ask for blessings and reassurance
Some kind of understanding to it all

Answers come in different forms
I know I was answered
I was sent a precious gift
A very special gift
YOU

The Twisted Tongue

*Many pages of my heart have been revealed
Though the thought of understanding passes me by
A whisper, a cry, a shout, or a scream
The words surround me with echoes*

*This heart it does beat so loud
A loudness to the chosen ears
This heart I wish I had instructions for
To the best ability I do use it
Thought of error and misuse are always on top*

*My words always fall short of explaining the heart
The tongue twists and the words tie within each other
Many times I've tried to find the chance
The chance to explain but the whispers are silent*

*As your back turns or the dial tone sounds
I wish I had done it correctly
The words that didn't sound or the ones that slur
Why I couldn't release what the heart holds*

*Will the heavens ever open and untwist my tongue
I pray that one day the shadow beside my walk
Will smile and understand
The value of the life that is hold within this is beyond gold*

Bless the heart and soul of this precious one

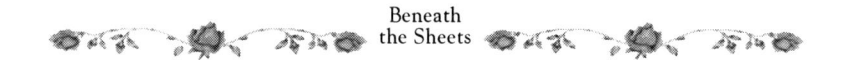

Unspoken Beauty

Have you ever seen the colour of a rainbow
The beauty of a sunset or yet the heavens above
The twinkle of the stars that lay over the night
Beauty, the unexplainable beauty

The colour of the inner soul
Let alone the flame that burns within the heart
The beauty within your smile
The inspiration of the words from your lips

Wings of the Angel that sits upon your shoulder
The breath of the almighty Lord that rests up above
A tear that rains down from the loved one in Heaven
Flickers of the candle when the spirit is present

The transformation of a caterpillar verses butterfly
Intertwining petals of a rose bud
Heated rays of a sun so bright
Formations of the clouds above

Viewing the world through roses
Allowing your heart to breath
You see a lot of unspoken beauty
Though never taking it for granted

Precious Moments

*Pitter patter on the water
Within the sac I play
Squirm and turn
Stretching and kicking while I grow*

*You shelter me and feed me with your love
You sing a lullaby with your heart's beat
Your giggles sooth me and reassure my safety
Every now and then you rub the wall surrounding me*

*I cannot see you but it is a natural bond we share
I know the ANGEL that speaks to me is YOU
Though I am tiny and the world is huge
The day will come that I can thank you
for every breath you give to me*

Beneath the Sheets

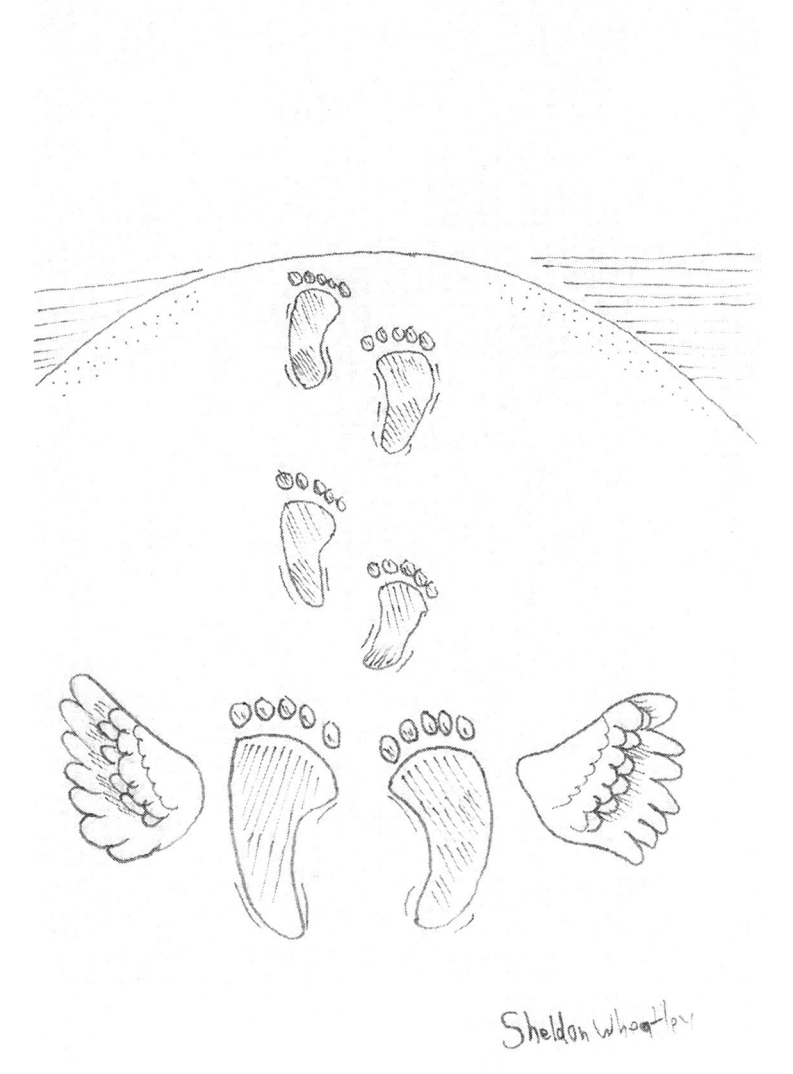

Sheldon Wheatley

Cinderella

Your heart crystallizes through your eyes
It's like a waterfall of emotions
When the sunshine rises all is illuminated
When the storms roll in
your brightness is covered by sadness

You are the centre of all
but yet you stand alone when in need
As gentle as a butterfly
As fragile as a rose
You listen to all
but never take another's hand for support

As strong as you stand, remember you count too

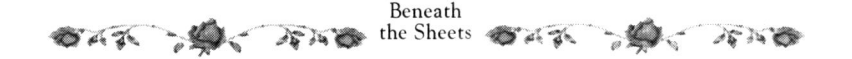

My Masterpiece

*Did you say Heaven or ecstasy
It's both with you my love
You are my Angel in Heaven
My partner in ecstasy*

*You tease me, you please me
My body is captured by tingles from your passion
My heart empowered by your love
My soul enlightened by the words that grace your lips*

*A masterpiece of the heart and soul
Our thoughts intertwine and complete each other
Our pages are in different hand writing
but they read the same
We are the answer to each others dreams*

We complete each other with a lifetime of love

The Mirror

The cracks of life
The circles of fear
The darkness surrounds the etching of your face
Sensations of emptiness shadow behind you

But through another's eyes
There are no cracks
The circles of life instead of fear
A rainbow of love surrounding you

Through each cloud there peers an Angel
Glorified with each step you take
They sing their praise
Dust you off at any stumble you may take

Beneath that wall there is a treasure
When that chest opens
The jewel that hides inside will shine so bright
The beauty it possesses and the love it creates are priceless

Close your eyes and close the past
Open the present and feel your heart
Believe in yourself and see the beauty within you
Answer the call of your love that is knocking from within

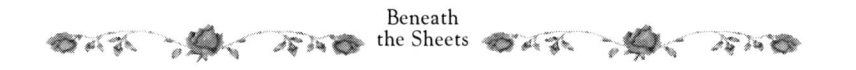

The Man I Love

The softness of his touch
The heat created by two bodies equaling one
The hypnotizing kisses
A lover of his own class

The sexy whispers
The tickling nudges
Warm embraces
Comforting words of love
A man of distinction

The beauty in his eyes
A wiggle to kill
Great buns that never stop
The man that fills my dreams

A Nightmare

I lay my head on my pillow
Begin to drift off into dreamland
Visions of you alone occur but wait, your are not alone
Who's with you

With a warm grasp you cuddle your lover
Bless her lips with the sensation of yours
Whisper sweet nothings and tell her you love her

Though, it gets dark and very cold fast

You break loose of the embrace
Look startled and puzzled
Say " it's over and goodbye "
Turn the other way and keep walking

There you leave your lover
Crying and helpless
She has no control of her emotions
So she reaches in her pocket
Then " slit "

A puddle of blood appears
She's gone

Beneath
the Sheets

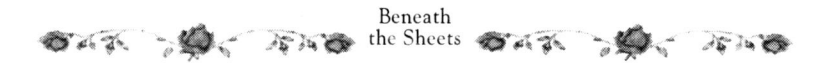

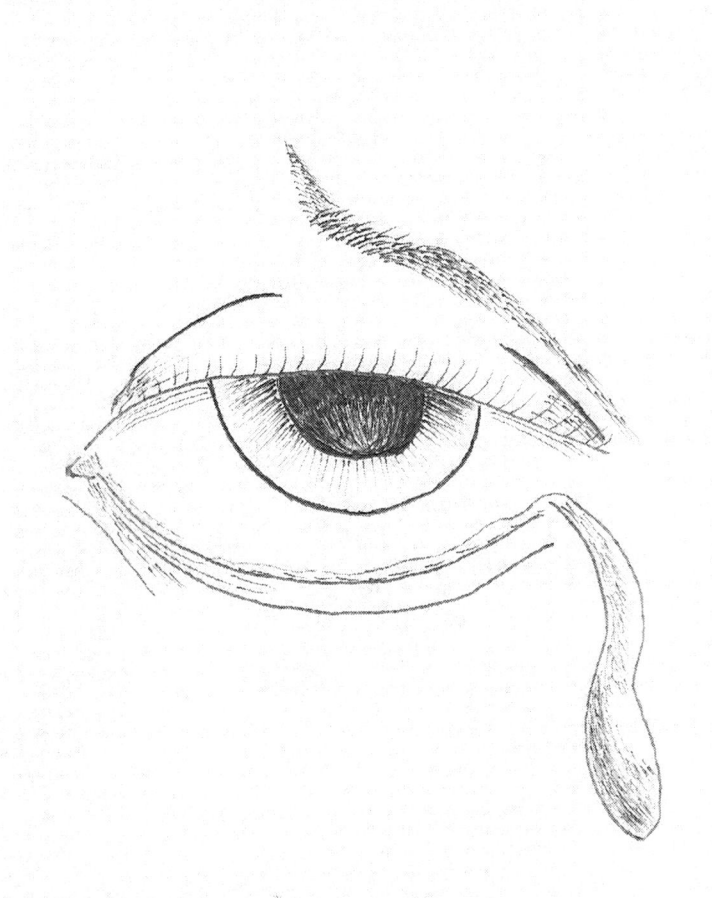

Sheldon Wheatley

A Lover Like No Other

*There I stand alone and helpless
No one around just jack frost nibbling at my nose
It was cold enough to freeze tear drops
Tear drops which were for my lover
A lover I remember and need
Though he's a lover like no other*

*I feel a warm grasp on my shoulders
I turn ignoring the tears falling
Unable to believe my eyes
There he stood
My lover*

*He warms me with an embrace of love
My lips become warm with the feel of his connecting
We whisper I Love You
Embrace hands
Agree to never leave one another again*

So off we went to somewhere warm

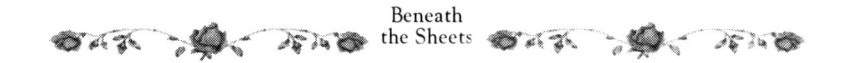

The Angel In All Of Us

*To the angel I never knew
To the angel I can see shining through his family
To the angel I hope to meet one day, I am here
Here to help the ones you love
To cheer and comfort them when in need*

*I never had the pleasure to meet you
Though I can see you through your family
You are and always will be
a special young man who is always loved*

*I ask you one thing
Though I may not be in your blood
Allow me to be an angel
and help watch over our loved ones*

Fulfilled But Curious

Loved but alone
Special but in the way
So close but yet an outsider
Feelings felt now

I'm wanting to understand
You show little by little

So secure yet so full of questions
Safe and protected I am
Loved so much
Needed and wanted
But why do I get the sidelines at times

My dreams are fulfilled with you around
The love I needed
The feeling of security
To feel sexy and yet a lady
To feel like gold instead of less
Should I be saying thanks

I'm not sure if you'll hear me
but I Love You with all my heart

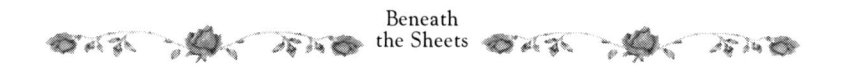

To Love Him Is To Dream

The magnetic attraction
The butterfly bellies
Blushing red cheeks
Warm thought filled heart
Farfetched wishes too good to have

A man I've always needed
A man I cannot have
A man I can only dream to love and hold

Thoughts of him away somewhere else empties my heart
When his calls are late or not there I worry
To hope he is okay and safe are constant thoughts

The best he deserves
Hurt he deserves not

Though to love him as my own is only a far away dream

Erotic Passion

To kiss ones lips
To share ones breath
To feel ones heart beat
The magic of another

The soft caresses
The gentle rubs
The security of his arms
Two bodies becoming one
The deep thundering passion
Thrusts of Love
Pure fulfillment

The erotic whispers
The feeling of your own world
Tension breaking giggles
Complete reassurance and comfort

A fantasy so long ago
Yesterday a dream
Today reality
Tomorrow my life

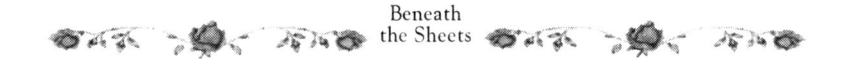

Little 8 Cylinder Camero

Stick shift or standard, I'm not sure
Great mileage and revving to go
Bumpers and head lights to stop traffic
The spot light of rush hour

The little camero of your dreams
The license plate empty
No key in the ignition but lots of gas to burn

A mileage meter still reading multiple numbers
The tires worn and hot
Yet no longer any tire tracks left or ground touched

Many times it seems as if that little camero
of your dreams isn't going to move
But be patient and cruise instead of drag racing
You'll find the correct license plate and key for the ignition

Sheri Celada

You Don't Understand

*It's stronger then it seems
More intense and important
Flickers are actually flashes
And sparks actually flames*

*Every moment more precious the next
A peck ?x! No actually a full fledged kiss
Warm embraces only hotter each time*

*Life starts with you and us
A dream of you now reality
Love growing faster than one knows*

*You're what I need
You're what I want
How to get it is the puzzle*

Beneath the Sheets

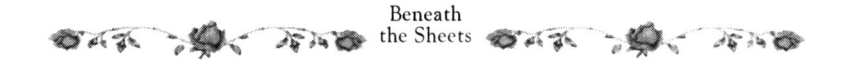

Sisters

Someone like you comes along only once in a while
Sisters like you are forever
The magic of the relationship is so special and beautiful

A tear
A laugh
A scream

No matter what we're always there for each other

Someone like you will always hold a place in my heart
Until the day I die I will always Love You

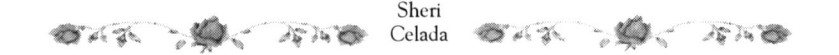

Pager Tag

Love messages
Sweet hellos
Curiosity of his whereabouts
All found on his pager

They seem to satisfy him
To cheer and comfort him
Though for her that's not always enough
More is needed to be said then little teases

Time is needed to say more but never enough time
Think things out
There is obviously pieces missing

Pager love is hand to handle and lonely at times for the sender

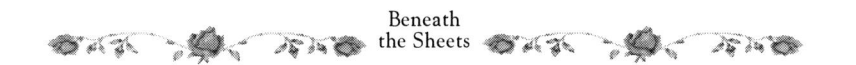

A Mishap

As I take your hand
Something in your eyes
Calls to mind
Sad goodbyes
I should have known better
I knew you weren't a fool
Now that you're gone
Pain is all I'll find

Running Doesn't Help

There I was alone and cold
I stand scared and off in thought
The rain blows my way and blends in with my tears
I look in the sky for a shooting star but no luck

I stand frozen like an ice cube
When suddenly a warm jacket
and a pair of arms surround me
Without thinking I turn to you
With tears running down my face

Our eyes connected
Thoughts flowed
The we hugged one another
Squeezed tightly and then slowly let go of one another

There was silence for a split second then
We both tried to speak at once
We were in such a hurry to explain ourselves

Then I felt an arm around me and a voice saying
" I Love You Baby"
Within a split second I returned the same message
Off we went arm in arm

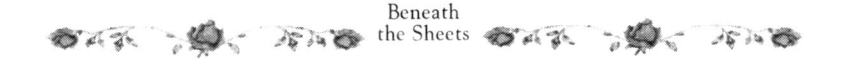

As Good As Gold

*Beautiful eyes of truth
Arms of warmth and security
Lips of soft, tender expressions*

*A heartbeat I feel through his touch and hear through his love
A mind of intelligence and organized thoughts
Manners and sensitivity of a real man*

*All of this and more make up a special person
A person who's everything a lady could need and more
He's one who knows how to treat a lady like a lady*

*Even the loneliest of times he can bring a smile about
My heart is full for him
An emptiness occurs when he's not there
It's another kind of feeling being with him*

I think it's called the beginning of love

Who's There

I walk the dark streets at night with caution
Constantly turning to look behind me
My pace is fast and silent
I hear weird noises as I walk

Do I turn to look and fall into a stranger's grasp
Or do I speed up and ignore the sounds
I speed up and walk right into trouble
As the street comes to an end it darkens

The sounds get louder and closer
I hear someone calling my name
and saying they're coming to get me
I hurry away to safety
Still to this day I wonder who was there

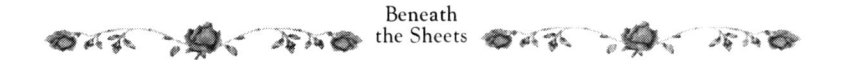

Two Becoming One

As two are becoming one
The moment warms
The bodies sticky and sweet
Skin to skin
With each caress we become closer and understand more
The beauty of each other is seen through another's heart

Each magical moment longer and hotter
Each caress drives one another
even crazier as the night progresses

His soft, delicate nibbles
His sweet kisses
Long gentle rubs
Closer we've become

If Tomorrow Never Comes

*Now I lay me down to sleep
If tomorrow never comes
Will you remember me
Or will I just be a face in the crowd*

*Will the laughs we shared be forgotten
The talks just an empty thought
Will your smiles become someone else's
Who's arms will hug you now*

*My heart will beat for you even from heaven
I will never forget your smile
You have branded my heart with such happiness
I long to see you again when our time crosses*

Thank you for lighting up my life.

Beneath
the Sheets

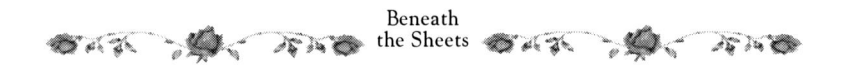

Sheri Celada